Histories,

Territories

and Laws

of the

Kitwancool

# Histories, Territories and Laws of the Kitwancool

## Second edition

**AS TOLD BY** the Gitanyow Hereditary Chiefs
to Constance Cox and B.W. McKilvington (Wee-ks-se-guh)
edited and with an introduction by Wilson Duff
with the Royal BC Museum
and a new foreword by the Gitanyow Hereditary Chiefs

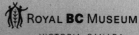

ROYAL **BC** MUSEUM
VICTORIA, CANADA

Histories, Territories and Laws of the Kitwancool, second edition

First edition published 1959
Published by the Royal BC Museum, 675 Belleville Street,
Victoria, British Columbia, v8w 9w2, Canada.

The Royal BC Museum is located on the traditional territories of
the Lekwungen (Songhees and Xwsepsum Nations). We extend our
appreciation for the opportunity to live and learn on this territory.

Cover and interior design and typesetting by Lara Minja/Lime Design
Cover photo of snow-covered Gitanyow totem poles, © Joel Starlund,
2010. Inside cover photos of Gitanyow territory, © Farhan Umedaly/VoVo
Productions 2021.

LIBRARY AND ARCHIVES CANADA CATALOGUING IN PUBLICATION

Title: Histories, territories and laws of the Kitwancool / as told by the
    Gitanyow Hereditary Chiefs to Constance Cox and B.W. McKilvington
    (Wee-ks-se-guh) ; edited and with an introduction by Wilson Duff with
    the Royal BC Museum.
Names: Duff, Wilson, 1925–1976, editor, writer of introduction. |
    Cox, Constance, 1881–1960. | McKilvington, B. W. | Royal British
    Columbia Museum, issuing body.
Description: Second edition / with a new foreword by the Gitanyow
    Hereditary Chiefs.
Identifiers: Canadiana 20220155674 | ISBN 9780772680327 (softcover)
Subjects: LCSH: Gitanyow (First Nation),—History. | LCSH: Gitanyow
    (First Nation),—Social life and customs. | CSH: First Nations,—British
    Columbia,—Gitanyow,—History. | CSH: First Nations,—British
    Columbia,—Gitanyow,—Social life and customs.
Classification: LCC E78.B9 H57 2022 | DDC 305.897/4128071185,—dc23

10 9 8 7 6 5 4 3 2 1

Printed and bound in Canada by Friesens.

MIX
Paper from
responsible sources
FSC C016245

100%

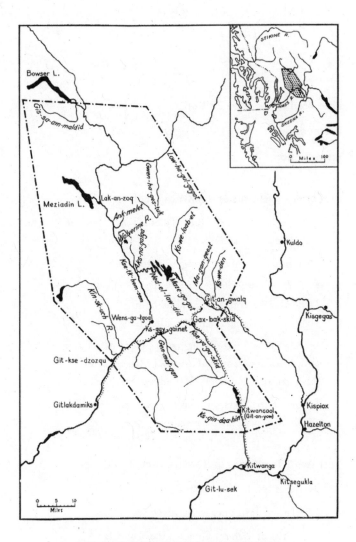

THE TERRITORIES OF THE KITWANCOOL.

FRED GOOD (NEAS-ŁA-GA-NAWS) MAP, UNDATED.

# Contents

PLATE I. KITWANCOOL VILLAGE, 1910.

G.T. EMMONS PHOTOGRAPH. RBCM PN04055.

## Foreword to the 2022 Edition

**In the year 2022,** some 63 years following the original publication of this book, our Huwilp, our Simgigyet'm Gitanyow (Kitwancool Chiefs) are still here, still grounded in the teachings of those featured in the 1959 publication, and still fighting to preserve our way of life, our territory in a sustainable manner, and the perseverance of our laws in the face of the relentless assault of colonialism in the form of the Indian Act, land dispossession and theft of resources from the Lax'yip.

For the Kitwancool—now reclaiming our name, the Gitanyow—our histories, territories and laws are the backbone of our culture as Gitksan people. Whether through research and writing, negotiation, litigation, direct action, or policy development, the teachings in this book still guide the work of the Simgigyet'm Gitanyow. Today, the Gitanyow Hereditary Chiefs Office serves as the administrative body for the Simgigyet'm Gitanyow, and for the Huwilp, on whose behalf they serve.

The Chiefs' names included in this book have since been passed on to the next generation, as they have for millennia. The names will live on, as do the responsibilities to the land, referred to as Gwelx ye'enst. As the new generation steps forward to carry on the traditions of the Gitanyow, we do so in the face of a climate crisis brought on by global colonialism and the industries which seek economic development at the cost of future generations' rights to the fish, wildlife, fresh water, medicines, mushrooms and berries which have sustained our people since time immemorial.

Reflecting back on the actions our former Chiefs and Matri-
archs took to document the histories, territories and laws of the
Kitwancool in 1959 in partnership with the Royal BC Museum,
it is this form of recognition of our system of laws and land tenure
that is missing today from the ongoing Crown denial of Gitanyow
title to the land. It is this missing recognition which has forced
the Gitanyow to the courts to seek recognition, despite the recent
adoption of the United Nations Declaration on the Rights of
Indigenous Peoples by both the Government of Canada and the
Province of British Columbia.

It can only be hoped and strived for, through continued edu-
cation and sharing of the knowledge contained herein, that when
our children and grandchildren republish this book in some
future form as yet unknown, they will be able to write a different foreword, based on a new path forged with non-Indigenous
society and governments.

Da'dilst Ayookx'hl Gitanyow: Our laws are still alive.

Naa dim si't yaa'kwis'hl wila l'awhl hla gyet'idhl Gitanyow:
Our system will not change.

Dax'gyethl gan da'dilsthl lax Yip: We are alive on the land.

Sim git litxw'hl hla gyet ihl Gitanyow ehl lax yip'dii't:
Gitanyow stand strong on their lands.

Gii'na'mehl UNDRIP gin'ax dim yuux'm dim dip gwin'ga'a'
dehl wila di'l'dilst'm: UNDRIP has given a way for us to show
we are still alive.

GITANYOW HEREDITARY CHIEFS

KITWANGA, BC

NOVEMBER 2021

PLATE 2. THE CHIEFS WHO RECORDED THE HISTORIES, 1958.

(Front row, left to right): Chief Wee-kha (Mr. Ernest Smith), Chief Less-say-gu
(Mrs. Maggie Good), Mrs. Constance Cox (interpreter). Second row (left to right):
Chief Gu-guł-gow (Mr. Peter Williams), Chief Gam-gak-men-muk (Mr. Walter
Derrick), Chief Gam-lak-yeltqu (Mr. Solomon Good). Rear row (left to right): Chief
Neas-ła-ga-naws (Mr. Fred Good), Chief Wee-ks-se-guh (Mr. B.W. McKilvington).

# Preface

**The authors of this book** are the Kitwancool themselves, for it contains their own statement of what they consider to be their histories, territories, and laws. It was their idea in the beginning that such a publication should be produced. The subjects dealt with are those which they consider important enough to include. The manner of expression, as closely as possible, follows their own. As editor, I have attempted to transfer their statements to the printed page with as little alteration as possible. I have also thought it desirable to add this Preface and a brief Introduction in order to make the material as meaningful as possible for the general reader.

The publication of this book is one step in the fulfilment of an agreement between the Kitwancool and the Provincial Museum of British Columbia. It is appropriate to begin by describing this agreement and telling how it came about.

In the spring of 1958 Wilson Duff and Michael Kew, representing the Provincial Museum and the British Columbia Totem Pole Preservation Committee, visited Kitwancool to negotiate the removal of a small number of totem-poles for permanent preservation. Discussions with representatives of the Kitwancool had been carried on in previous years, but up to that time no totem-pole had ever been removed from the village. The Kitwancool chiefs did not consider it proper, under any circumstances, to sell their totem-poles outright.

Accordingly, we made a new kind of offer: that for each old pole which we removed for preservation, a new and exact copy, carved in Victoria, would be returned and erected in the village. A meeting of the chiefs and people of Kitwancool accepted this proposal, but added one further condition: that their histories, territories, and laws were to be written down, published, and made available to the University for teaching purposes. Since that described precisely one of the functions the Museum is trying to perform, we were happy to agree.

The following agreement was drawn up and notarized: —

## AN AGREEMENT
### between

## THE PEOPLE OF KITWANCOOL AND THE PROVINCIAL MUSEUM OF BRITISH COLUMBIA CONCERNING CERTAIN TOTEM POLES OF KITWANCOOL

Whereas   The Provincial Museum of British Columbia desires to preserve a number of the totem poles of Kitwancool for the use and benefit of future generations of both white and native peoples, and

Whereas   The people of Kitwancool also desire to preserve their totem poles and furthermore desire that their authentic history, the stories of their totem poles, their social organization, territories and laws be written down, published and used in the highest educational institutions of the province to teach future generations of white and native students about Kitwancool,

The parties hereby make the following agreements: —

The people of Kitwancool hereby agree:

1. To permit the removal of three totem poles to Victoria, B.C. for permanent preservation. The three poles being:
   a) Chief Wiha's pole now lying beside the house of Mr. Walter Douse.
   b) Chief Wiha's pole now standing in the old village.
   c) Chief Guno's pole showing three frogs and now fallen in the old village.
2. To provide authentic information on their history, traditions, social organization and laws to properly qualified persons, so that the information may be written down, published and used in teaching students about Kitwancool. In future to provide such information as is required to properly qualified representatives of the University of British Columbia so that they may further clarify questions which may arise in the course of studying and teaching about Kitwancool.
3. That the conditions listed below, to be undertaken by the Provincial Museum of British Columbia are acceptable to them.

We certify that these conditions are acceptable

Chief Wiha                          Chief Gamlakyelt,
                                    per subchief Leseq

The Provincial Museum of British Columbia hereby
agrees: —

1. To cause the above described poles to be removed from
   Kitwancool, to transport these poles to Victoria, B.C.
   for permanent preservation, to have skilled carvers make
   exact copies of these poles, to transport the copies back
   to Kitwancool, construct for them suitable bases and
   erect them in places to be designated by the Kitwancool
   people, and to accomplish this by May 30th, 1959.
2. To provide funds to cover the expenses of a person acceptable to both parties to visit Kitwancool for a period of not
   more than two weeks, to write down the authentic stories
   of the totem poles and the history and laws of the Kitwancool people as dictated by them. (As Mrs. Constance Cox
   has been named as a suitable person we agree to contact her
   and determine whether she is willing and able to undertake
   this work, and if so, to make arrangements for her to do so.)
   It is understood that copies of the information so written
   down will be made available to the people of Kitwancool,
   the University of British Columbia, and the Provincial
   Museum of British Columbia.
3. To borrow the map of Kitwancool territory prepared by
   Mr. Fred Good, to copy it, and to return the original
   map to Kitwancool.
4. To issue a publication which will embody the information and map referred to above, in sufficient numbers so
   that it may be obtained by all who are interested.

5. To provide the University of British Columbia with copies of all of the above information and map, and also sufficient copies of the above mentioned publications for the use of professors and students. Furthermore, to recommend to the officials of the University that these materials be extensively used in teaching the coming generations of students about Kitwancool. And furthermore, to inform the officials of the University that the people of Kitwancool would welcome suggestions for the improvement of their legal position and welfare; and in future may ask the University and the Provincial Museum for information and advice on matters within their competence and concerning the people of Kitwancool.
6. To provide copies of this agreement, for permanent record, to the people of Kitwancool, the Provincial Museum of British Columbia, and the University of British Columbia.

Wilson Duff,  
Provincial Museum  
of British Columbia.

Walter Derrick,  
Chief Councillor,  
Kitwancool Band.

Hazelton, B.C.  
March 24, 1958

W. Bailey,  
(Authorized under  
the Indian Act  
to administer oaths.)

Witness:  
Peter Williams,  
President.

In accordance with the agreement, arrangements were made for Mrs. Constance Cox, a former resident of the Hazelton area who speaks the Indian language fluently, to spend some time in Kitwancool during October, 1958, and to record the histories and laws as dictated by the chosen representatives of the Kitwancool people. The procedure to be followed was written down in the following statement, which was sent to all parties concerned: —

To the people of Kitwancool:

According to the terms of the agreement signed in March, I now have the pleasure of sending to you your old friend Mrs. Constance Cox, who was chosen on your suggestion as the most suitable person to write down the Kitwancool history and laws. I am sure that you will give Mrs. Cox your full cooperation in carrying out the difficult and important task which we have assigned to her.

May I offer the following suggestions on how this work may best be carried out. As a general principle I assume the people of Kitwancool know what is important in their history and traditions. They know what should be written down and they know who the best speakers for each clan are. Therefore, the choice of topics to be recorded and of speakers should be left completely to them.

The first step, then, is for the people to decide what things should be written down. Presumably this will include the full stories of the three totem poles sent to

Victoria, the full histories of each clan in the village, the stories of other totem poles, the story of the Tsetsaut war, and other information on Kitwancool history, laws, and customs. In recording a story, it is very important to get it as complete as possible, including even parts involving adultery or other things that are regarded as offensive. The whole story should be written down, and offensive parts can be left out at a later time if necessary.

The second step is for each clan or family to appoint a spokesman to sit down with Mrs. Cox and relate the histories. This must be done slowly enough so that she can write down a full and direct translation at the time. It will be slow work, but will ensure an accurate transcription.

When Mrs. Cox returns her notebooks to us, we will have the stories typed out and copies will be sent to the University and to Kitwancool. Preparations will be made for turning out a publication which will satisfy the terms of the agreement.

Mrs. Cox spent the period from October 10th to October 19th in Kitwancool. Her work was much facilitated by the generous hospitality and cooperation of Mr. and Mrs. B.W. McKilvington (Mrs. McKilvington being the school teacher in the village). As the appointed chiefs narrated the stories, Mrs. Cox translated them into English and Mr. McKilvington wrote them down. The narratives fill one hardcover notebook. On the last page appear the signatures of all the chiefs who were responsible for the telling of the histories. The list is as follows: —

These are now the signatures of all these chiefs who have been responsible for the telling of these histories:

| | |
|---|---|
| Wolf Clan Chief: Wee-kha | Mr. Ernest Smith |
| Wolf Clan Chief: Gwass-ɫam | Mr. Walter Douse |
| Wolf Clan Chief: Gam-gak-men-muk | Mr. Walter Derrick |
| Wolf Clan Chief: Neas-ɫa-ga-naws | Fred Good |
| Wolf Clan Chief: Wee-ks-se-guh | B.W. McKilvington |
| Frog Clan Chief: Gam-lak-yeltqu | Solomon Good |
| Frog Clan Chief: Less-say-gu | Maggie Good |
| Frog and Wolf Chief: Gu-guɫ-gow | (President) |
| | Peter Williams |

Mr. Peter Williams is the President of Kitwancool and has been given the power of attorney to handle this business concerning the Wolf poles of the double headed Gaa-qukdik-giat and the Skim-sim, and the Frog pole of Chief Gwen-nu named Nee-gamks. Mrs. Constance Cox was the interpreter and Mr. McKilvington wrote the stories.

The manuscript was prepared in typewritten form and submitted to the Kitwancool for their approval. It was returned in November 1959, with a number of minor corrections and additions, including the lists of personal names in the Appendix. The corrected manuscript was then prepared for publication.

Handwritten accounts taken down phrase by phrase from an interpreter require a certain amount of editing to transfer them into an easily read printed form. Punctuation and sentence structure often have to be revised and minor misunderstandings cleared up. The spellings of Indian names always present problems, because the language uses unfamiliar sounds which are not rendered accurately by the ordinary letters of the alphabet. In general, the system used by Mrs. Cox and Mr. McKilvington has been retained. When the same name is spelled in a variety of ways, one has been chosen and used throughout. One minor change has been made: the surd *l* (pronounced approximately like *th* and *l* run together) is shown with the symbol ł rather than by means of *l'l*.

Care has been taken to preserve the original mode of expression. The order of the material has been altered slightly; for example, to bring all the laws and customs together in one section. The map incorporates the information shown on the one drawn by Mr. Fred Good (mentioned in the Agreement). The photographs used in Plates 1, 3, 5, 6, and 7 were taken by G.T. Emmons in 1910 and are reproduced through the courtesy of Dr. Viola E. Garfield. Plate 2 is from a photograph by B.W. McKilvington; those in Plate 4 were taken by the writer in 1952.

The debt of gratitude which the people of Kitwancool and the Provincial Museum owe to Mrs. Constance Cox and to Mr. and Mrs. B.W. McKilvington should also be placed on record here. Their efforts, generously and freely donated, have been largely responsible for the accomplishment of this task.

WILSON DUFF.

PROVINCIAL MUSEUM, VICTORIA, B.C.,

DECEMBER, 1959.

# Introduction

by Wilson Duff

---

**The Kitwancool** (kit— "people of," wan— "place of," łkul—
"small" or "narrow") are a small Indian tribe whose village,
also called Kitwancool, is located on a tributary of the Skeena
River near Hazelton, British Columbia. Justly famed for its totem-poles and its coolness toward intruders, the village until quite
recently was accessible only by trail. Today it is readily accessible
by road from Kitwanga, 15 miles to the south on the bank of
the Skeena, in the mountainous country of the Coast Range,
about 150 miles from the coast. Beyond the village to the north,
the road is passable by jeep or truck for a short distance, then
reverts once more to a trail, the famous "Grease Trail" to the Nass
River. Continuing on, the trail passes Kitwancool Lake (wrong-
ly called Kitwanga Lake), crosses a low divide to the Cranberry
River, and leads to the upper reaches of the Nass itself.

The Kitwancool might be said to belong more to the Nass
than to the Skeena, for their territories extended far to the north
and, in fact, included more of the Nass Valley than was held by
the Nass tribes themselves. In earlier years the village, with its
large community houses and its forest of totem poles, was mainly
a base of operations, occupied during the winter months when

the important social and ceremonial affairs of the tribe were carried on. Many of the affairs required the presence of people from the other villages on the Skeena, and it was an advantage to have the village fairly close to theirs. But for the greater part of the year the Kitwancool moved through their Upper Nass and Upper Kispiox territories fishing, hunting, and trapping.

Their closest relatives, however, are the people of the Upper Skeena, and the Kitwancool are usually classified with them to form the Gitksan (git— "people of," ksan— "Skeena River") division of the Tsimshian. The other Gitksan villages are Kitwanga and Kitsegukla on the Skeena nearby, Gitanmaks upriver at Hazelton where the Bulkley joins the Skeena, Kispiox at the junction of the Kispiox and Skeena, Kisgagas on Babine River, and Kuldo even farther up the Skeena. These seven tribes share a single dialect of the Tsimshian language, distinctly different from the dialects spoken by the Niska of the Lower Nass and the Tsimshian of the Lower Skeena and Coast. It is said, however, that the Kitwancool formerly spoke the Niska dialect, which would not be surprising considering their close ties with the Nass.

No matter how others may choose to classify them, the Kitwancool think of themselves as an independent and completely autonomous tribe. In matters which affect the tribe as a whole they insist that nobody else has the right to speak for them. Some such feeling of tribal unity is characteristic of the social structure of all the Tsimshian, but the Kitwancool have cemented it still further in recent years by taking formal steps to unite the clans and by appointing a president.

This attitude of independence has been expressed most clearly with reference to "The Land Question." The Kitwancool insist that they have never been a party to any agreement to relinquish any of their rights over their territories. They have never made a treaty, nor have they been conquered. They have never admitted that the Government has any right to set aside plots of and for them as Indian reserves. In their view, all of their former territories still rightfully belong to them.

Most of the materials in this book could be said to back up this claim in one way or another. First, the "histories" of the clans are themselves the traditional statements of rights to certain territories, which are accepted as valid by the other clans. The totem poles stand as visible symbols of these histories (which were related whenever a pole was erected), and in a sense are considered as legal deeds to the territories concerned. Second, the account of the Tse-tsaut wars tells how the tribe acquired the territory around Meziadin Lake. Finally the territorial claims and concepts of ownership are stated in explicit terms in later sections of the book.

The following brief outline of the social structure of the Kitwancool will assist in setting the accounts which follow into context. Essentially, the Kitwancool tribe is made up of members of two matrilineal, exogamous phratries—the Wolves and the Frogs. These are called "clans" in the manuscript. Formerly a third phratry, the Fireweeds, was weakly represented in the tribe, but its members did not own any of the tribal territories. The Wolves consist of three groups which have separate histories and own separate territories. In native terminology these groups are called "houses." They have no names other than the names of their chiefs. These segments of the Wolf phratry in order of their rank are: —

w 1: Wee-kha, Gwass-łam, Wee-skim-sim, etc.
w 2: Mah-ley, Neas-ła-ga-naws, Ak-gwen-dasqu, etc.
w 3: Hai-zimsqu.

The first of these was the largest group; in fact, it was subdivided further to give two more "houses," those of Wee-lezqu and Tka-waaku. The third is regarded by some as part of the second.

The Frog "clan" is also made up of a number of ranked segments having separate histories and territories: —

F 1: Gam-lak-yeltqu, Low-khone, Shen-dił, etc.
F 2: We-dak-hai-yatzqu, etc.
F 3: Gwen-nue, etc.
F 4: Yak-yaaqu, etc.

Here again the exact number of "houses" is a matter of interpretation. F 1, for example, was originally one, but in later time split to form two.

There is no single chief of the tribe; each "house" acts under its own chief. However, the chiefs are ranked in their social standing, and the highest ranking Wolf chief and Frog chief claim a great deal of respect from the others in their phratry and take the leadership in matters of common interest. Highest ranked of all is the leading Wolf chief (now Wee-kha, but formerly Gwass-łam); nevertheless, he is not in any real sense the chief of the whole tribe. It was presumably to compensate for this lack of unified leadership that the Kitwancool have established the office of president.

The manner in which the ranking of the chiefs is revealed in their seating arrangements at feasts is explained in the manuscript. In a similar way, the ranking of the houses in the village was shown by their locations. This is illustrated in the panoramic view of Kitwancool in 1910 on the cover.* Six houses are shown—three Wolf houses on the left and three Frog houses on the right. From left to right they were the houses of W 3, W 2, W 1, F 1, F 2, and F 3 (the groups named above). In other words the leading Wolf chief and leading Frog chief lived side by side in the centre of the row, with their fellow chiefs in descending order of rank toward the ends. Actually this ideal arrangement did not extend the complete length of the village. There were other houses farther to the left (south) and these included two Frog houses placed there presumably because their own end of the village did not offer suitable sites.

The Kitwancool tribe, then, represents an amalgamation of several groups of people of different origins. The traditional histories of the most important of these groups are the subject of Part One of this book. The first is the story of the leading Wolf group (W 1), of their early home on the sea-coast at the site of the present Prince Rupert, of their travel up the Nass River, and their establishment in their present territory. The second, dealing with the Nee-gamks pole, tells how Gwennue and his people (F 3) tried to find their way back to their ancestral home of Dam-la-am on the Skeena after the flood had carried them west to Alaska, and of their adventure along the way. Next, the story of the Ha-ne-laɫ-gag pole traces the travels of a band of Interior people from the headwaters of the Skeena (F 1), tells how they took possession of much of the Upper Nass, and finally came to form part of the tribe. The same group is the one most involved, also, in the early episodes of the Tse-tsaut wars.

---

* Plate 1 in the 2022 edition.

Neas-la-ga-naws' account of the Wolf group of Mah-ley (w 2) tells how they left their relatives at Gitanmaks (Hazelton) to move up the Kispiox River, then split up again and joined the Kitwancool, bringing their Upper Kispiox territories into the tribe. Together with the account of the Tse-tsaut wars, these accounts comprise most of their history, as the Kitwancool know and tell it.

Very little information about the tribe appears in old historical records or journal. They lived too far from the coast to meet the maritime fur traders, and were remote from all the fur trading posts. They were relatively late in coming into direct contact with Europeans.

They first appear in the official census records in 1889, with a population of 195. Before the Tse-tsaut wars and the introduction of white man's diseases they must have had several times that number. In the 1880's and 1890's many of the tribe decided to move to the Lower Nass, where missionaries had established new settlements. At times the old village must have been almost abandoned. In 1903, for example the Indian Agent enumerated only 68 there, another 115 having taken up residence on the Nass. In recent years, however, the number in the village has grown rapidly, from 90 in 1939 to 173 in 1958. Today Kitwancool is a vigorous community with a day-school, village hall, and church, and a reputation of industry and independence.

PLATE 3 (*facing*). WOLF CLAN TOTEM-POLES, 1910.

Left: Pole of Skim-sim and Will-a-daugh. Right: Pole of Gaa-quk-dik-giat.

G.T. EMMONS PHOTOGRAPH. RBCM PN03817.

## PART ONE

Histories

of the

kitwancool

# Historical Story of the Totem-Poles of the Clan of the Wolves, Gilt-winth, of Kitwancool

Recorded on October 11th and 13th, 1958, from Chief Wee-kha (Mr. Ernest Smith).

**The figures on the first totem-pole** (left, in picture) are as follows: The bird on the top is the Giant Woodpecker (Wee-get-weltku); the figures around the top of the pole are the house carvings; next is the large bird Skim-sim, the mountain eagle; fourth is a row of carvings representing children or small people, the ones who fish through holes in the ice (the holes may be seen in the front of the house); the figure at the bottom of the pole, holding the child, is the important figure Will-a-daugh.

The name of the pole is Skim-sim and Will-a-daugh. On these two depends the history of the pole. It holds many legends of the clan, one of which will be recorded as follows.

The story begins a thousand years ago, more or less, at Ke-an (the present Prince Rupert), where the clan had its village. The chief had many nephews and nieces. One of the nieces of the chief went out to gather wood. She found a wood grub of the kind that eats pines. She had a child from this grub, and she put it in a wooden cradle and stood it up against the wall. She sang the baby a lullaby (lim-ath-a-now), about its little hands which were moving all the time. The child was, of course, supernatural, and the hands moved all the time like those of a human child.

Unknown to the mother and the chief, the grubworm child had eaten its way through the wood of the house and had reached underground to the next house, where it was eating the walls, boxes, and everything of wood. It went underground to house after house, and the people could not understand what was eating everything up. Just a part of this "child" was doing that.

The people in the last house at the end of the village decided to keep a watch on their wooden boxes. They heard a gnawing noise in one box and found that it was a huge wood grub. They stabbed and stabbed it and dug a trench following its huge body, stabbing each part as they uncovered it. They followed it right back to the baby in the cradle leaning against the wall. The trench they dug can still be seen near Prince Rupert, by anyone who knows the story.

The mother felt very sad at the loss of her child. She went down to the edge of the water and cried over its loss. She made a wish that the water would rise and flood the village. However, the only person drowned was herself, Will-a-daugh.

The people got together, and the chief decided they would move. They moved to the Nass River (Nish-gah) and made a village which they called An-lath-gauth-u, which means to see in both directions. After the village had been established, the chief and his family went up on the mountain to hunt groundhogs (queak-u). On the mountain, a groundhog spoke to one of the young hunters, saying "hea-uk, hea-uk." It was telling him that his wife was being unfaithful to him; the word "hea-uk" means "she is at it again." The young hunter left the people on the mountain and secretly went down to the village. He arrived late at night when it was very dark, and found his wife asleep in bed with another man. The boards of the wall were only tied on with roots, and he pushed them aside, entered, and killed the man.

He looked at the man he had killed, and saw that he was a prince, the son of a great chief. He wore chief's clothes. His blanket or robe was trimmed with ermine skins on one side and marten skins on the other, from the shoulder to the bottom of the robe, about 8 inches apart. Along the bottom between the skins, were unborn caribou hoofs. (A likeness of this robe has been preserved right up to this day as the ceremonial robe of the Wolf clan.) The chief took the robe off the dead man, with the intention of keeping it, but as he stood holding it he heard a voice calling to him.

It was the mother of the dead prince weeping and asking for her son back. The son was really a wolf, the Prince of the Wolves, who was impersonating a human being. His name was Ga-ba-gam-kwen, meaning one who killed and ate ten deer at a time. He also had a second name, Gam-gak-men-muk, meaning one who bit off the ears of the deer and ate them. (Mr. Walter Derrick now carries this name. It is a very valuable name, worth many hundreds of feasts.) The mother kept crying and asking that her son be given back to her, "If you do not give my son back, something terrible will happen to you."

The figure of a large bird on the totem-pole is the mother of the dead prince and holds the history of the pole and also the funeral song of the Wolf clan. As this bird flew over the village, she was crying "Give my son back," and singing the death song: "Lou-see-tee-au, Lou-see-tee-au, łqu-łquu."

Then the bird spoke: "If you do not give me back my son, something dreadful will happen to the village."

The chief spoke: "Give her back the robe of her son, the robe you kept."

She would not take it from their hands. They put it on the roof, but still she would not take it. She kept flying over the village singing the funeral song. Then she sang a funeral song calling for heavy rain (ho-ho-wis) to punish the village. It began to rain very hard, until streams ran through the village.

The chief decided that they would have to move again. They moved farther up the Nass River and made a new village on the bank of a small river called Zam-an-lu-tool ("protected river") (the name compares it to a head covering). The chief and members of his household examined the hills, valleys, and mountains to see if it was a suitable area to live. During this inspection of the country they camped by a beautiful spring of clear water.

The chief's name was Gwass-łam ("borrowing a shin bone"). His niece was Zo-gam-doa-gasqu. His nephews were Lu-lo-gam-hud ("in the water went the frogs"), Gan-na-um-zem-qwanks ("frogs sitting in the spring of water"), and Za-gam-yousqu.

They saw something strange at the bottom of the spring, like a box with figures carved on it. The chief sent his three nephews to bring it to him to examine. They examined it but could not understand what it was except that it was a square looking box with figures carved on it.

After examining the box they again heard the voice crying "Give me back my son or something dreadful will befall this village." The dirge was repeated again and again.

The chief took the box and examined it more closely. He found that it represented a house, which was built as though it had a basement of rock (dhak-gam-loab). In each of the four corners was a carved bear. All this time the bird was crying "Give me back my son. If you don't, something dreadful will come to all of you." He held the box up over the fire. She stopped crying and spoke: "Nothing will happen to you, as I have got my child." She did not take the box.

The chief kept it and passed it on, along with its name dhak-gam-loab, to the present day as a coat of arms or crest.

The chief decided they would move again. He gathered his household and travelled until they reached Git-an-yow. That was the first name given to this village, and means "village of many people," or "big village." It was 15 miles long, extending from 6 miles below the present village up to the lake. Later they began having wars, and after the wars there were very few people left, and they changed the name to Kitwancool, which means narrow valley.

Regarding hunting and trapping grounds of the Kitwancool, Chief Wee-kha (Mr. Ernest Smith) explained: —

They travelled around to find a place where there was much food—meat and fish in the forests, lakes, and rivers—so they could live there forever. They found the place Git-an-yow, and found it to be very wealthy in game and fish and furs. When other nearby villages learned of the good place the Git-an-yow had found, they came and joined the village also. They decided that the proper thing to do was to build houses, and three were built.

The houses they built were so big that two smoke-holes were made in each house. The small figures shown on the totem-pole (in the picture) were used as house carvings. The name of the house was An-wi-sin-zock, which refers to its large size. A visitor entering the door had so far to go to the back of the house that he was ashamed or embarrassed (zoak).

The two totem-poles (in the picture) both belong to the same crest and have the same stories. The crests on the second pole are the same crests brought from Prince Rupert as the designs for the totems to be carved at Git-an-yow. These were the crests used in Prince Rupert a thousand years ago by the Wolves.

Monday, October 13th.

## The History of the House of Skim-sim, the Mountain Eagle (continued)

**This story begins** from the creek of Kse-gen-daa-hin, near the present village of Kitwancool, where the tree was cut to make the pole.

On top of the pole is the double-headed man called Gaa-quk-dik-giat. The death song of this pole must be sung at the time of the erection of the new pole of this house. (Mr. Walter Derrick is singing this song. It will be recorded on a tape recorder at the time the new pole is erected.)

A "death song" is sung when a chief passes away. His body is laid out ready for the funeral, the house is filled with people from all the different clans, and then the death song is sung. Until it is sung the history is not completed. All the members of the clan pay money for this funeral. The honour and power are explained in the song, and it is sung in honour of the departed chief.

(Mr. Derrick, Chief Gam-gak-men-muk, says he feels quite sad when he sings this song because it has the history of the past and the history of his family.)

The two poles stand side by side, both belonging to the same house and representing the same power in the house. There are always two chiefs to hold the power of these poles, just as there are two heads on the pole. They are picked out as young children to hold the power of these poles, and always attend when the chief holds council meetings so they will know what to do when their turn comes to take over the power of these poles. Chief Wee-kha (Mr. Ernest Smith) is still living, and holds the power of the poles, but has given it to his nephews Mr. Walter Douse (Gwass-łam) and Mr. Walter Derrick (Gam-gak-men-muk). When he passes, the power will go to these two brothers.

In a chief's house you always sit in the same place, according to your stand or rank in life among the people. This house, unlike other houses, has two seats for the chiefs, in accordance with the two heads on the pole.

In feasts, many sit like a council for the chief. The chief will make a suggestion and they will decide on what the chief wants done. Hundreds of names belong to this house. It would take too long to write them down now, but we promise that when the poles are returned by the Government to Kitwancool, we will write all these names and have them ready to hand to the anthropologists at the raising of the new poles. In a council or meeting, if guests are invited from other villages, they are seated according to their power and rank as chiefs.

This pole (No. 1) was the first pole erected in Kitwancool by the clan of the Wolves. It had been erected about a thousand years ago near Prince Rupert. When a pole decays (a pole lasts about 200 years), or at the death of a chief, a new pole is always erected in the same place. When these people migrated, they took along duplicates of their totem-poles and erected them in their new permanent villages.

When a pole is erected or changed, it is erected at the same place. A feast is always given and the territories are discussed. They tell the people the size of their village, the mountains they own, their hunting and fishing grounds. They tell this so that each new generation will know what they own. The new chief and his council divide the land. They tell each clan which mountains they can have, and what areas they can hunt and fish in.

PLATE 4 (*pages 18–19*). DETAILS OF THE SKIM-SIM POLE, 1952.

WILSON DUFF PHOTOGRAPH. RBCM PN10413.

## 2

## Historical Story of the Nee-gamks
## Totem-Pole Belonging to the Frog Clan

Recorded on October 13th and 14th, 1958.

---

**Before the flood** (before Noah built his ark), Chief Gwen-nue (whose present successor is Mr. Godfrey Good of the village) built an ark (raft) and got on it with all his family. They left his village, which was 8 miles or more in length and named Gid-da-gan-gh, and floated away on the flood-waters. They drifted for months, and when the flood subsided they landed on the coast at a place called Git-ha-guns north of what is now Ketchikan, Alaska, where there was dry land.

They camped there for some time, but did not like the place. They made up their minds to return to their original village. They had lost the route by which they came, and got lost by going up Alice Arm to a place called Kits-auth. Finding they had made a mistake, they returned and camped at Kincolith for a while.

From this mistake they took a name, Lu-hiss-yet.

They kept on with their journey and went up the Nass River, which was called by them Liss-ims. At each place they stopped something would happen to them, and from it they would take a name. A boy's name, Galey-ges-gau-tqu, means travelling, and then stopping.

Still travelling, they came to a place where people were living, called Lak-hane-gul. As they came close they paddled very slowly, as they did not know who the people were, and were afraid of them. A man in the village did hear the dip of the paddles, but did not investigate, and they passed quietly by. They made a girl's name from this—Galey-ks-oat-qu, which means "the quiet dipping of the paddle."*

After they passed this village it became very cold, with ice on the river. They put aside their paddles and used poles, and from this they made a boy's name, Gwal-did-thou. It means when they put the poles in the water, water froze to them.

Continuing on, they came to a place which they named Git-ha-guns, where they made a village of brush houses for the winter. When spring came the sister of the chief very mysteriously disappeared. The people looked for her, but could not find her. They stayed at this camp for a long time, and many babies were born there.

Frog children were also born, and two small ones carrying one another arrived at the chief's (their grandfather's) house. He came up the trail, and as soon as the little frogs knew it was their grandfather, they went to meet him. He picked them up in his hands and carried them to the step of his house. The little frogs would not leave, staying under the step. Later the chief took them into his house. He sat down at the back, where the chief always sits, and they went and sat down beside him. The

---

\*    This is name is now to be given to Mrs. Ann McKilvington by Chief Gwen-nue because she was so quiet while this history was being written.

little frogs tried to crawl up on his lap, and he stooped down and lifted them up.

The chief, grandfather of the little frogs, called in all the wise men and wise women to try to find out why the little frogs wanted to stay with him. One of the frogs kept saying "Ze-weed, Ze-weed," and the one on the other leg kept saying "Ga-dath, Ga-dath." These were the names their mother had given them. The wise people could not tell what they were saying or why they were there.

They called a very very old woman from the village. She recognized the names the little frogs were saying, and then she knew that the chief's sister had been taken by the frogs and was married to one. One of the little frogs said "ha-libis," and the old woman said, "Nee-gamks wants to borrow a ha-libis (awl)."

They gave an awl to the little frog. He took it in his mouth, took the smaller frog on his back, and went away. Their grandfather followed them a long distance to the lake. They looked back and saw their grandfather, then went into the lake.

The chief then knew where his sister had been taken. He gathered the men of the village and they dug a ditch and drained the lake. They stood ready to grab the sister as she came out of the lake. Then a flying frog came out of the lake, and as it flew by a chief stabbed it. That man kept it as his crest. When Nee-gamks rose out of the water she was riding on the back of her husband, the chief of all the frogs, with her frog children in front of her. As she rose she sang the funeral song (which will be recorded when the Frog pole is raised in 1959). The song is called Lemk-ks-goax-qu Nee-gamks meaning "they floated out of the water." She is the figure shown on the top of the pole.

After she sang the funeral song, she gave it to her brother. It was impossible for her to return to her brother as she had taken on the form of a frog, and she asked to be left with her frog husband as he was very kind to her.

The Chief Frog was very nicely formed. His eyebrows and lips were the colour of gold, as were the nails on his hands and feet. The man was going to kill him but his sister spoke: "Do not kill him. I will tell you all the good things he has done for me."

She showed her brother her frog children sitting with her—one named Ga-dath, the other named Ze-weed. She told of all the kindnesses the Chief Frog had done for her. She said that she was never going to come back, as she was going to stay there with the Frog. She sang a song for her brother and gathered in her beautiful long hair, which floated on the water.

Her brothers left and went home to Ks-gay-gai-net ("upper place"). (That is an ancient settlement on the north bank of the Cranberry River right at the canyon, at Mile 58 from Kitwanga. There is a large graveyard there.) They made a pole with her likeness on the top and the frog children below, and her father put up a pole in her honour.

They value the pole (the one taken to Victoria) very highly, as it represents the lost sister and the nieces and nephews of the clan. This pole was made by Chief Ak-ǵwen-dasqu, which means "it is forbidden to touch him," and is a name belonging to the grandfather of Mr. Rufus Good and his family.

These people headed in the direction of Kitwancool, heading for their own original village, Dam-la-am ("flat prairie place"), on the north side of the Skeena River about 10 miles west of Get-an-maks, where there are small farms today. They came to a place about 3 miles north of Dham-Kitwancool

(Kitwancool Lake). Here they built a house out of burned logs calling it Wilp-am-dauh meaning house of charcoal.

They travelled on very slowly, camping for several months in some places, but always back toward their original home. They sent the young men on ahead to look over the country, and they found it good.

Finally they came to Git-an-yow. They found people living here (which brings the date to several thousand years later). When they arrived in Git-an-yow, they made a great feast and invited all the surrounding villages, then erected this pole in memory of their sister, Nee-gamks. That is the name of the pole. Thus they have always used a frog as their clan crest.

PLATE 5. THE NEE-GAMKS TOTEM-POLE
OF THE FROG CLAN, 1910 (LEFT).
G.T. EMMONS PHOTOGRAPH. RBCM PN03816.

# 3

## History of the Totem-Pole Ha-ne-laɬ-gag ("Where the Raven Sleeps With Its Young")

This history was recorded on October 15th, 1958.

---

**Present were** Chief Wee-kha (Mr. Ernest Smith), Chief Gu-guɬ-gow (Mr. Peter Williams, president of Kitwancool) Chief Neas-ɬa-ga-naws (Mr. Fred Good), Chief Gam-gak-men-muk (Mr. Walter Derrick), Chief Less-say-gu (Mrs. Fred Good). Chief Less-say-gu was the only one with the power to discuss the history of this pole, and she signed over this right to the male members present. Chief Gam-gak-men-muk said that he was honoured to be given the opportunity of telling the history of this great pole.

This pole, standing in front of Albert Douse's house, is one of the most important in the village and is the pole that ties the other poles together. It holds the power for the other two poles (in the photograph); in other words, it represents all three poles, and is the pole of the Raven.

Now begins the story of this most important pole. Shen-diɬ was the name of the chief, and Zem-an-lu-sqaks, meaning "wading in water," was the name of the place they came from. In their travels they reached a grassy mountain named

Sga-nest-sun-habausq ("mountain of grass"). They went along the top of the mountain to the other end, which had timber, and gave it the name Lak-wee-yep. When they left the mountain, they came to a river flowing south, named Anuk-gemelik-nagag or Wolverine River. Looking back, they could see the grass mountain and they felt a great deal of sorrow in their hearts and they sang their first funeral song, Gam-lu-gał-dal-good, referring to the heaviness of their hearts. They sang it because they were leaving that country and felt very sad.

They came to another river, Aks-na-galga meaning "river of poor water." They asked Chief Galga if he drank this water, and he said "yes" and that is why they gave the river that name "waters of Galga." They had a ceremony and put their power on that river and land, which meant that it belonged to them as they had found it first.

Again they travelled on and reached Wens-ga-łgul, a long, very narrow valley. When Chief Shen-dił had taken the land there and had left their power there, they travelled on again. They reached another river which they named Ks-gay-gai-net, meaning "river above." It was a good salmon-fishing river in a good country; they built a permanent village here and put their mark on the river, thus claiming ownership of it. Then they thought they would move on and see more country, so they fastened up their homes and left.

They found another place and built another village, at Lak-getk-kse-dzozqu, meaning place of the seagull hunter. The name of the seagull hunter was Shin-ge-win; his mother's name was Aks-lak-amks, meaning "clear waters at a nice prairie-like place." The chief built a house, and on the door (which was suspended by a thong) was carved a frog, the crest

of the people. The name of the door is Gan-naw-om-lak-ptoor ("frog on the door").

Once more they moved, leaving their power and mark which made this country theirs, and returned to their former village Ks-gay-gai-net. The reason they were travelling so much was that they were making their map, and on each piece of land when they stopped they had left their mark and power, making it theirs. Still travelling, they arrived here at Git-an-yow (now Kitwancool) by following what is now the Cranberry River (Ks-se-ya-ga-sked—"river that descends gradually"). When they arrived, the clan of the Wolves was already here. The Frog clan decided to build a house close to that of Gwass-łam; it was built in the same style as the first house they had built at Zem-an-lu-sqaks ("place of wading"), and was given that name as a house name. The chief was Shen-dił, whose name refers to the frayed clothing of those who had travelled so long and far.

On the top of this pole (on the left in the picture) is the nest of the Raven, showing the young ones sitting on each side. It is called Ha-ne-łał-gag ("where the Raven sleeps with its young").

The carving at the foot of the pole is the mountain eagle. It was loaned to the children of Wee-kha and Gwass-łam (Wolf chiefs), and carved on this Frog clan pole to give them some honour. If this house should be built again, or the pole replaced, they would not carve the mountain eagle on it.

PLATE 6. THE HA-NE-LAŁ-GAG POLE
OF THE FROG CLAN, 1910 (LEFT)
G.T. EMMONS PHOTOGRAPH. RBCM PN04033.

This history is taken from a picture (see Plate 6) belonging to Chief Gam gak-men-muk, who kindly loaned it for this purpose. In the same picture is a pole with carvings of some men on it. The name of this pole is Gaydom-gan-alah, meaning "pole resembling smoke." It is taken from the second pole belonging to the house with the frog on the door.

The chiefs established themselves at Git-an-yow and raised their poles. The poles gave them their power or coat of arms and gave them the right of ownership of all the lands, mountains, lakes, and streams they had passed through or over and camped or built villages in. The power of these poles goes unto the lands they had discovered and taken as their own. The power from the house of this chief and his council goes as far as Getk-kse-dzozqu, the place of the seagull hunter, and includes Ks-gay-gai-net, the "upper fishing station." The power of the pole still goes on and belongs to Shen-dił. Belonging to him also, as a gift, is Wens-ga-łgul ("narrow place").

## History of the Lands Belonging to Chief Neas–ła–ga–naws (Mr. Fred Good), or the History of Mah–ley and Ak–gwen–dasqu of the Wolf Clan

Recorded on October 19th, 1958, from Mr. Fred Good.

**These are historical stories** which were handed down to us by our fathers and great-grandfathers. The names of the two chiefs are Mah-ley, meaning "something that was crazy" (however, nothing was really wrong with the man), and Ak-gwen-dasqu, meaning "not permitted to be touched." These two chiefs held the power; when they gave out orders they were obeyed. A chief holds the power over each household, and a household is not just one family but may include as many as thirty families.

This household originated from the house of Spookqu at Get-an-maks (Hazelton), the great-grandfather of Mr. Fred Good. They left this house and travelled up the Kispiox River. They came to a place called Geth-sqan-snard and camped there for many years.

One year, when the season came around for the hunting of beaver, two brothers went hunting together. They were Ak-gwen-dasqu and Galey (meaning "outside noise"). As they were opening a dam, the force of the water knocked Ak-gwen-dasqu down and he was killed. The other brother did not understand what could have caused this misfortune, and returned to Geth-sqan-snard. Since he was the bearer of bad news, he did not go right into the camp. He went around to the back of the house where his brother's wife slept. When he got close to the wall, although it was in the middle of the night, he heard voices, a man's and a woman's.

When he heard the man's voice talking to his brother's wife, he knew what had been the cause of his death. He was so upset that he went back into the woods. No one in the village yet knew what had happened.

The next day at mid-day he went back to the village and entered his house. His mother asked him why he had come home alone. He did not tell her that his brother was dead, but answered: "He liked the place where he was. He was having good luck and he didn't want to come home." His mother then gave him a meal. Later, when they were sitting by themselves, he told her in a whisper that his brother was dead. He did not want the rest of the household to know the bad news, and he told his mother not to cry or the others would find out.

When night came and all had gone to sleep, the mother went to sleep as well. All of a sudden she burst out crying. Her son Galey asked her, "Why do you cry?"

"I had a bad dream," she answered. "I dreamt that your brother was knocked down under the dam by the force of the water and is dead."

"He is having good luck hunting," Galey said. "It is not right for you to think these things."

Everyone was asleep in the household except Galey. He was listening for something. Then he heard the two voices again, talking together. Soon the voices stopped, and they too went to sleep.

Very quietly, Galey crept over to where the man was sleeping with his dead brother's wife. He killed this man and left the body lying in the woman's bed. When daylight came and the household woke up, the killing was discovered. The dead man was a relative of Galey's, and this fact made it very difficult to settle the trouble.

They decided to divide into two groups, which would go to different places. The head man himself headed for Kis-ga-ga-as. The other group went to Get-an-gwalq, about 60 miles from Kispiox, at a canyon. The name means "you are always thirsty there." Five chiefs were in this group—Mah-ley, Ak-gwen-dasqu, Galey, Haiz-emsqu, and Lega-gal-well. When they reached Get-an-gwalq, they made a permanent camp there. They had left some of their people at their last village, Geth-sgan-snard.

After they had built their permanent village at Get-an-gwalq, two brothers went out to hunt bear. Their names were Galey and Ak-wen-dasqu (a boy had taken the name of the previous Ak-gwen-dasqu, who had died at the beaver dam). They were at the place where the two rivers met, the Ks-wee-den and Ks-get-an-gwalqu, watching for bear. A very large grizzly bear with two cubs appeared and entered the water. The cubs sat on her shoulders, one on each side of her head, and the mother bear swam across toward the men. In the middle of the river she got into very swift waters. One of the cubs fell off her shoulders and was drowned. When she reached shore in front of the men with one cub, she turned and looked into the water and cried, almost like a human, for her drowned baby. After she cried she sang a death song.

A totem-pole still standing in Kitwancool has the picture of this grizzly bear, and this pole holds these stories.

(Mr. Fred Good sang the song.)

After the brothers learned the song, they shot the bear with their bows and arrows. After that they sang the funeral song.

The place where this happened is the boundary of the upper part of the Kispiox River, which belongs to all of Mr. Fred Good's people. They marked this boundary by singing this song at the place where the two rivers meet. This boundary adjoins that of Gwass-łam of Kitwancool. The lower part of the river belongs to the Kispiox people.

These lines run north-west. The proof of ownership of these lines dates back thousands of years, to include all the lands, mountains, rivers, creeks, lakes, ponds, valleys, timber, minerals, and oils.

Then two more boys, nephews of Chief Haiz-emsqu, went out to hunt. They went to a mountain called Lip-ha-head-tqu, which means standing alone or independent mountain. Up this mountain the two brothers shot a caribou. It was very cold and a blizzard was blowing. The older boy, Zex-al-al-gak, was skinning it and the younger boy stood looking on. It was so terribly cold that he froze to death. When the older boy found that his brother was frozen, he, too, sang the death song. (Mr. Fred Good sang the song at this point.) This death song proves the ownership of this mountain rests with Chief Haiz-emsqu and his whole household. Haiz-emsqu stands below Chief Mah-ley, who is the high chief, but they stand together.

The time had come to divide the lands. They were all camped at Get-an-gwalq and deciding on the hunting-grounds. They put a head man on each piece of land.

Maze-go-gat Lake, now called Swan Lake, is the headwaters of the Kispiox River. Another river is called Ks-we-loabet.

On farther was a piece of land called Gwen-ha-ges-tuk (meaning "lakes"). Chief Ak-gwen-dasqu was put in charge of this place and of Low-ha-gholl-gag-gat. (It must be remembered that Chief Mah-ley was still head chief over all the rest.)

On another piece of land was a lake named Ned-del-law-did. This name means "two close together"—in this case two lakes. Mah-ley put Galey there as head man.

Chief Mah-ley, the head chief of all, was in charge of Get-an-gwalqu and also of Mah-gan-geest, which was the stream where the man got crushed under the beaver dam when it broke. The headwaters of this stream came from the mountain where they hunted goats and groundhogs. At this place they built a house, which they named after the mountain Gahal-la-łmatik, which means "the chest of the goat."

Then Mah-ley called two young men and told them to climb the mountain Gahal-la-łmatik to look over the land and see what was at the back of the mountain. When they reached the top of the mountain they looked down and saw a river, and smoke coming from houses away down below. When it was getting dark, they went down and came to the village of Gwass-łam. They saw also the brush huts of the girls, who were forbidden to walk about during the fishing season. They threw stones at these huts.

The names of the two boys were Uks-gam-dham-mass, which means "just hugging" (the frog), and Ghaw-gweah. The men of the village told Gwass-łam, and he called out in a loud voice that they were to come to him.

They went into the house, and Gwass-łam gave them seats and food. They told him that they had been sent by Chief Mah-ley to see what they could see in the way of other lands. Then Gwass-łam remembered the words of Spookqu: "If you happen to see any of my people, call them to you." That is the reason he called these two young men.

So Gwass-łam sent back word to Mah-ley to come and stay with him. When the word came, they at once packed up and went to where Gwass-łam was living, a place called Ghax-bak-skid, at the 50-mile point from Kitwanga up the Kitwancool Valley, past the lake. The two houses of Gwass-łam and Mah-ley joined together and became as brothers, and Gwass-łam was very pleased. He told the newcomers that he had a large permanent village at Get-an-yow and invited them to join him there.

The whole village then went. and when they arrived in Get-an-yow, Gwass-łam showed Mah-ley where to build his house, beside his own, on the east side. They built the house there. They were very grateful to Gwass-łam for his kindness in asking them to come and live with him as brothers.

After the house was built, they decided to have a feast. They invited all the chiefs of Kitsegukla and Kitwanga, and they came with all their relations. When the guests arrived, they were shown a pole which had been erected. It was called Spe-leg-en-esqu, meaning "grizzly bear's den." On this pole was shown the grizzly bear with her cubs, as was seen at the junction of the two rivers when the mother grizzly lost her cub. This is the coat of arms or crest of the house of Mah-ley.

The feast was to show all the surrounding tribes that the house of Mah-ley now belonged to Git-an-yow. Chief Gwass-łam got up and told the assembled people that the house of Mah-ley was now accepted by him and that all were now Git-an-yow people. In front of all these people, Mah-ley then spoke and said he would honour this and accept the grizzly bear as his crest, honouring it as the prince of all bears. The grizzly-bear totem-pole stands at the end of the village of Kitwancool. (Mr. Fred Good now sang the song of the sitting grizzly of stone, now seen near the south end of the village.) At the ceremonial dances the chiefs wore grizzly-bear skin to honour the memory of this grizzly bear.

## History of the Wars with the Tse-tsaut: How the Village of Git-an-yow Became Kitwancool

Recorded on October 16th and 17th, 1958, continuing on from 3.

**Also present the second day** was Chief Gam-lak-yeltq (Mr. Solomon Good).

The people had arrived here at Git-an-yow, bringing their poles, and the power came with the poles and went into the land.

The chief of Git-kse-dzozqu came to Wens-ga-łgoal, to visit his brother Shen-dił. He wanted to marry his brother's daughter, his own niece. This was against the laws, and Chief Shen-dił refused to give his daughter to her uncle. The latter went back to his own village, but named the day when he would return and renew his request to marry his niece.

When that day approached, Shen-dił took his daughter and went away to the river Gen-meł-gan, which was reached by crossing (the Cranberry) at Ks-gay-gai-net. They travelled up that river to a mountain, where they camped and hunted groundhogs. While they were away, his brother arrived at

Wens-ga-łgoał. All he found there was Shen-dił's wife, who had remained behind. He kidnapped her and took her to Git-kse-dzozqu. She did not want to go, but knew she would be killed if she didn't.

(According to a former definition, the name of this village was derived from the Tse-tsaut word "zohzqu" meaning "a place where the people got their spring water for drinking and cooking.")

Shen-dił arrived back at the village with his daughter and found his wife gone. All he found was a male slave, who told him, "Your brother has taken your wife away to Git-kse-dzozqu." He told the slave to go and bring his wife back. He was not angry with her or with his brother.

The slave went to Git-kse-dzozqu and told the woman he had come to take her back to her husband. The brother asked him, "What did my brother say when you told him I had taken his wife?"

"He did not say anything. He just bowed his head. But he told me to go and get his wife," the slave answered.

The slave returned home without the woman. Shen-dił then said: "You will go back and I shall go with you." He took up his club, made of caribou horn and carved to represent his crest, the Raven. This was the highest weapon used for war, and was used only in the hands of the highest chief.

When Shen-dił opened the door, his brother stood with his head bowed. He hit his brother on the head with the club and he died right there. Then he took his wife, who went willingly with him. As they departed, he sang a "weeping song" for the loss of the brother he had killed. (The name of this [type of] song is lem-mik-oie. Chief Walter Derrick chanted this song for his brother when he died.) A little farther on he sang another song lem-mik-oie. (Both songs have the same name, but one is sung in a sadder way. Every Frog pole has this song; it will be sung at the raising of the pole in 1959, as has always been the custom when raising a Frog pole.) Just as he was nearing Wens-ga-łgoał Shen-dił sang the third and last song, lem-mik-oie which is named Ghed-lqul-hel-len, meaning "loneliness in memory of the ancestors." Then they reached their village, Wens-ga-łgoał, and lived there.

Every year the people of neighbouring villages used to come to Git-kse-dzozqu, and they would laugh and dance. The visitors were Tse-tsaut people, and when they got to the hill nearby, they would dance and yell to see if they were welcome. Then Shin-ge-win, a head chief in the village, would go up a ladder on to the roof near the smoke-hole. He wore a head-dress filled with eagle-down which represented peace and friendship. (If someone fights with you, he will come next day and put eagle-down on you, and you must not fight anymore.) He would send out a lot of eagle-down on his visitors. Then they exchanged presents, the Tse-tsaut people giving furs in exchange for food, which was very scarce with them. This custom was kept up for many years.

But the next time the Tse-tsaut came to exchange furs for food, they got a very cold welcome. Only a very small amount of eagle-down was blown upon them, and when they saw so little eagle-down, they knew there was trouble in the village. They went down to the chief's house. All they found was an old woman, Oks-lakamks, the mother of Shin-ge-win. "Has our brother died?" they asked. "Yes," she replied. "He has been killed by his brother, Shen-dił."

They asked her how the lines went so that they could follow the people who killed their brother. They asked the way to Git-an-yow so that they could go there and kill them off. The old woman told them, and when she had finished they killed her. They put her upon a roasting-stick and prepared her for roasting and left her there. They then decided to make war against the Git-an-yow people and became wild and belligerent. Then they went back to their own country beyond Meziadin Lake and waited for the time the old woman had told them the people would be in their village.

They planned to attack in March, which was called Ha-owalq ("forbidden") because that is the month when black bears are born, and it is forbidden for a mother-to-be to look at a bear at that time or else her child might be disfigured.

The Tse-tsaut started out on the war-path in March, when there was much deep snow, and came by the routes told to them by the old woman. They came along the ridge of the mountain We-lak-ha-bas-qut (Grassy Mountain). Looking down they saw the [Kitwancool] lake, and smoke was rising from the houses along the edge of the lake. It was the smoke from the fires of the Git-an-yow people, who were on their way to their hunting-grounds. Two of the Tse-tsaut warriors put on wolf-skins and came across a short distance on the ice. The Git-an-yow people were camped on the south-west side. They looked over at these animals, watching their movements, and knew they were not real animals. It was getting dark, and the Tse-tsaut kept in hiding.

Just as it was getting light, the Tse-tsaut made their attack on the sleeping camp. They knocked down and burned all the brush huts and killed everyone. One young girl escaped across the ice at this end, but they chased her and killed her. They left her there with the arrow sticking in her back.

A young man named Ze-gho-zec from the village of Git-lu-sek (near Cedarvale) was engaged to this girl, and he was coming to the village to see her. When he found that she had gone out with the hunting party, he did not stop to camp but kept on to try to catch up with them. When he reached the lake, he saw something dark on the ice. It was a body, and lifting it up he found that it was the body of the girl he was to marry. He examined the snowshoe tracks (Tse-tsaut snowshoes were different from theirs), and found that the Tse-tsaut had attacked the Git-an-yow. He crossed the lake to the burned camp and saw what had happened there.

He went back to Git-an-yow, where only the old people had remained, and told them that their people had been killed. Then he went home to Git-lu-sek. The young man's father called a meeting, and nearly all the people who came were from Git-an-yow or had relatives there. They decided they would wage war on the Tse-tsaut and avenge those who had been killed. These relatives lived at Kitwanga, Kitsegukla (Skeena Crossing), and Git-lu-sek. To the able-bodied men who were to help them in the war, they gave their young women, out of gratitude. These three villages banded together under the orders of the big chiefs, and the Git-an-yow chief agreed that this should be done, thus making it lawful. This was done very soon after the massacre, as they camped on the shores of the lake.

The avenging party followed the snowshoe trail of the Tse-tsaut. The captain of the party was Ze-gho-zec, and his father also went as a warrior. As they travelled they saw where the Tse-tsaut had camped, with four (horizontal) poles around the fire on which it was the custom to rest their feet and dry them. Before they camped the captain would go out to see if the enemy was near, and they were careful not to make any noise until he told them that the enemy was a long way away. At last they caught up with them at a place called Lak-an-zoq, which means place for fishing village. Far ahead they saw the smoke of their enemies' fires. They made war clubs and other weapons and planned a night attack. They knew they would find the Tse-tsaut asleep with their feet up on the racks and planned to break all their legs as they slept. They went on without eating or sleeping to catch the Tse-tsaut during the night.

The captain went on ahead to see what the enemy was doing. He returned and told them he had found them camped at Lak-an-zoq, asleep. Just before dawn they made their attack, and killed them all and won their battle. During the battle they had bands playing music. Then all returned to their homes.

**THE SECOND WAR**

Not long after this war the Tse-tsaut made another war attack. There were now enough people left in Git-an-yow to make up an army. Some of them lived at Ks-gay-gai-net, 58 miles from Kitwanga.* Several years had passed and the Tse-tsaut were continually giving trouble, trespassing on the Git-an-yow hunting grounds.

The Tse-tsaut came down and made an attack on the people of Ks-gay-gai-net. These were Low-khone and his wife, who

---

* Mileages along the trail from Kitwanga to Aiyansh were measured by a white man, Mr. Robert Jennings, in 1911.

was the daughter of the chief of Kitsegukla and a sister of Kook-shan. They had a son, Gham-logh, and a daughter, Na-gay-eł. These two children had been told what to do in case of an attack: if they saw the village in smoke, they were not to join in the battle but to run away and go right to Git-an-yow and report what was happening. In this attack, Chief Low-khone and Chief Gam-lak-yeltqu were killed. The children returned to Gitan-yow and told the people of the attack and that the two chiefs had been killed.

It was decided to have another war on the Tse-tsaut people. Chief Gwen-nue (the name means "begging") made the plans and asked the same villages as before to come and join them. He invited all the strong young men from these other villages, and they had a council and a feast. They were given clothing for the battle, and also were given young women of the village as a reward for coming out to go to war. A young warrior may be unwilling to go to war, knowing that he may lose his life, so they give him something to fight for. The arrangements were completed and two captains were picked out to lead them—Chief Gwen-nue of Git-an-yow and Chief Ks-shue of Kitsegukla, nephew of Kook-shan. They set out to find the enemy.

The Tse-tsauts had taken as a captive the wife of Gam-lak-yeltqu, named Low-tkal-dhow, meaning "frozen in the ice." She was a sister of Mah-ley. Knowing that the Git-an-yow warriors would chase them, she left a trail of pine branches on the hard frozen snow. When she could not find any brush, she chewed alder bark until it turned red, to mark the way for her rescue. When she had no more bark or branches, she used grouse feathers.

The Git-an-yow war party had two men on guard always, and when they stopped to camp, these men went on ahead as scouts to see if the enemy were near. If they saw no sign, they returned and made camp. They travelled on and knew they must be very close to the enemy. The scouts went on ahead, through open country, and came to a hill below which was a big lake called Meziadin Lake. They saw smoke and saw the enemy camp on the lake. It was approaching evening and they stood still on the hill, looking down on the enemy camp, their arrows crossed in front of them to resemble branches. The enemy saw them but thought they were trees. When it was quite dark, they glided away and went back to their own camp to report what they had seen. When they came into the light of the camp-fire, they carried their arrows in a special way and the look on their faces was the same as when they had found a grizzly bear's den. They told their story to their father and described the enemy camp.

Chief Gwen-nue, who was also a powerful medicine man, talked to the party and told them what they must do. They were to do just as in the previous war, and use just the same weapons to hit the enemies over the head. Captain Gwen-nue gave orders for them to sing, and while singing to rush with their spears toward a big hemlock tree and hit it. If it fell down, it was a sign that they would win the war against the Tse-tsaut. This was done to give encouragement to the warriors, and they were strong enough to knock the trees down. They started out to face the enemy. The captain told them to have strong hearts, for they were going to win. They reached the hilltop from which the scouts had seen the enemy camp, but kept among the trees. Gwen-nue said, "We will now sing a song wishing for a fog to come down thick enough to hide us from our enemies." The fog did come down, like a smoke screen, and everything was dark. The plan was to attack under cover of the fog. If the enemy discovered that they were surrounded, Gwen-nue was to give a loud shout and they were to attack immediately.

Gwen-nue led his warriors across on the ice and they began to surround the enemy camp. The Tse-tsaut had strung a line around the camp, hung with things that would rattle at a touch and wake them up. Not knowing this, Gwen-nue brushed against the line and it rattled. The Tse-tsaut chief began to sing and shake a rattle to waken his warriors. Gwen-nue shouted out to attack at once. The battle was fierce, but the Git-an-yow people finally won.

The Tse-tsaut head man, Gein-ne-glay, was like a witch-craft doctor and they could not kill him. Every time they stabbed him, he rubbed his hand over the wound and made it well. He had a magic spear which lengthened so that he could reach anyone he was stabbing at. He could not walk as the bones of his legs had been broken in the battle, but he sat and thrust his spear. He did not kill anyone, but he did wound badly An-nak-aws of the Git-an-yow Wolf clan, the son of Ne-gah-gah-lugh and a relative of Gam-lak-yeltqu.

Back in their home village, the women of the Git-an-yow fasted and put on mock battles every day while the warriors were away, to bring good luck and success to the war party. Only one woman in the village refused to join in these mock battles. Her name was Gax-dee-modqu, the wife of An-nak-kaws, and because of that her husband died in the battle.

Just before the witchcrafter Gein-ne-glay died, three black-bear cubs appeared most mysteriously about him, no one knew from where. Then he died. Captain Ks-shue from Kitsegukla was also very severely wounded in the battle. He wanted to show the people that he, too, had power. He asked them to mix some mud with water in a bucket and he drank it. Asking them to be very quiet, he told them that if they heard a noise from his stomach like a beaver slapping the water with its tail, he would survive.

The battle was over, and the Git-an-yow people had won. Their reward was the lands in the region of Meziadin Lake; this was the price of the Git-an-yow blood lost in these battles. On their return home after this battle, they changed the name of Git-an-yow to Git-win-łqouel. With the great losses they had suffered, they found they had few people left and their village was not large anymore. That is why they changed the name to Git-win-łqouel, which refers to the smaller number of people. (The white people cannot pronounce this name, and it is now pronounced and written Kitwancool.)

It should be noted that the father and grandfather of Chief Wee-kha (Mr. Ernest Smith) fought in the war between the Tse-tsaut and the people of Git-an-yow, and his grandfather was killed in the war.

### THE TSE-TSAUT

The Tse-tsauts came from beyond Meziadin Lake. They were people who never had a permanent home, and when they found a land or something they wanted, they at once made war to get it. As we see, they warred many times against the Git-an-yow people. They now have a village 100 or more miles beyond Meziadin Lake, near what is now Cariboo Hide on the Stikine River.

## PEACE CEREMONY AND LATER INCIDENTS

After the war and the renaming of the village, they gathered together with the Tse-tsaut and swore an oath to make peace. The name of such a gathering is Ghawa-gharney. The Tse-tsaut people promised they would never make any more attacks on the Kitwancool people. Any violation of this law was unpardonable. All was now peace among them; they all went out on their hunting-grounds, and the young men went out to hunt for furs.

By this time the white people had arrived in Telegraph Creek and the Hudson's Bay Company had a store there. The Tse-tsaut bought gunpowder from the Hudson's Bay Company and came down and met the Kitwancool at a place called Lak-an-zoq. Up to this time the Kitwancool had used only bows and arrows, spears and war clubs, but now they bought guns from the Tse-tsaut, with whom they were at peace. A band of Nass River people came to this meeting at Lak-an-zoq. The Stikine people did not have a very kindly feeling for these people because a few years before the Nass people had killed one of the members of the Stikine band of the Tse-tsaut. The Stikine people felt as though they should take revenge. They told the Kitwancool chiefs: "You had better leave. Our hearts are not very kind toward the Nass people. Do not stop to camp, just keep travelling to your own village." The Kitwancool chiefs were Tka-waakq and Hai-zimsq, and their nephews were Aw-will-yep and Alga-gams-getqu respectively, all of the Wolf clan.

After warning the Kitwancool to hurry back home, the Tse-tsaut helped them to cross the Nass River below Meziadin Lake. The part of the river that runs through the lands of the

Wolf and Frog clans is called Ks-tkhem-sim. On their way homeward they came to a stream with many steelhead salmon, called Ankmelet. When they saw the fish, they were tempted to camp and catch mel-let (steelhead). They camped here only one night, but the Nass people caught up to them and camped beside them. These were the people against whom the Tse-tsaut were planning revenge, and, unknown to them, the Tse-tsaut surrounded the camp during the night and were sitting around on the hills watching. In the morning the Kitwancool people left their camp and went on toward their own village. A short time later a gun was fired off toward them by the Tse-tsaut, and the two chiefs, Tka-waakq and Hai-zimsq, were killed. The other members of the party, including the two nephews Aw-will-yep and Alga-gams-getqu, kept travelling on as quickly as possible, running away from trouble.

They came to a very large pine-tree and hid in a hole underneath it. Another nephew named Oowelkqu slid down into a canyon and hid among the rocks near the water. The Tse-tsaut were watching and called out where the young men had hidden. One Tse-tsaut man named Shan-neik walked along the tree with a spear in his hand, jabbing it down among the branches and brush and listening. He heard the two boys crying. He was also of the Wolf clan (the Tse-tsaut Wolf clan). "Don't cry, no harm will come to you. I will guard you here," he said. The other Tse-tsauts went down into the canyon where the third boy had gone. As they looked down, the boy rose up to look around and they saw him. They shot, and the bullet hit him slightly on the chin. He fell into the water and floated a short way down-stream, then got out again and escaped.

The Nass man against whom the Tse-tsaut wanted revenge had meanwhile slipped away and hidden. He travelled back to his own village safely.

The two boys who had hidden under the pine-tree escaped and headed toward Kitwancool. They arrived safely after dark, and brought the word to the relatives of Tka-waakq and Hai-zimsqu of what had happened. The people went back and cremated the bodies of the two chiefs. When they reached the place, they found the bodies laid out with bear-skins over them, which showed that the Tse-tsaut were sorry for having killed chiefs with whom they were at peace. The Kitwancool people so appreciated this act of kindness that they did not retaliate for these murders. After the cremation they returned to their village.

About a year later the Kitwancool were again at one of their camps, called Ks-gay-gainet, when a body of Tse-tsaut, including many women appeared. They again wanted to make peace as was done before and invited the Kitwancool people to go with them to Lak-an-zoq, in the land of the Tse-tsauts, for the ceremony. The invitation was accepted, but when they got to Lak-an-zoq there was nobody there, and the Kitwancool became a little suspicious. Then the Tse-tsaut said the peace talk would be at Aw-wee-zah, near what is now Bowser Lake. They sent four young men to lead the Kitwancool to this place. Aw-will-yep and Algagams-getqu planned to accompany two of these Tse-tsaut men to Aw-wee-zah, but the big chief and the rest of the Kitwancool people stayed at Lak-an-zoq along with all the Tse-tsaut women. The Kitwancool were told by one of the Tse-tsaut boys that if they went to that place of gathering, they would have no chance of returning safely.

The two young men who had gone on with the two Tse-tsaut toward Aw-wee-zah camped, cut wood, and made cooking fires. The Tse-tsauts put some meat on to cook, but took it off before it was cooked signifying that they were once more going to commit murder. The two boys knew they were going to be murdered that night. After they had eaten the half-raw meat, they made a plan to save themselves. They decided to cook the Tse-tsaut a good meal and after the meal give them tobacco to smoke to stupefy them and put them into a heavy sleep. While they were asleep, the boys would kill them and escape. They prepared a place for the Tse-tsaut to sleep near the fire and filled their smoking-pipes again and again. Finally the Tse-tsaut fell into a deep sleep. Their guns were under their heads. Quietly the boys slipped the guns out from under the pillows, put the muzzles right on the chests of the Tse-tsauts, and pulled the triggers. One of the enemy, although shot, escaped and climbed into a tree. They waited until he came down, then killed him with a spear. This was how they saved their lives. They left the dead Tse-tsauts where they lay and returned to the big camp at Lak-an-zoq. One of the boys went ahead, stood on the edge of the river, and gave the call of the wolf. They crossed in a canoe, each carrying one of the ball-and-cap muskets taken from the Tse-tsauts. In the camp were the two Tse-tsaut chiefs and their women in addition to the band of Kitwancool people who had come to attend the peace meeting.

When they heard the call of the wolf, the people in the camp knew that all was not well. The Kitwancool people at once surrounded the camp. One of the Tse-tsaut chiefs, knowing he would have to die, asked permission to dress in his chief's clothes so that he could die as a chief should. He dressed and then sat still, not speaking. The Kitwancool were hesitant about killing him; then a man from outside the circle leapt forward with a hatchet in his hand and split his head open. This man who killed the Tse-tsaut chief was Thgal-k-datqu (meaning "one who unknowingly slept on a frog") of the Wolf clan. The other Tse-tsaut man was also killed, but the women were taken back to Kitwancool and cared for. One by one these women ran away. They were allowed to escape.

After this, from time to time the Tse-tsaut people would come to Kitwancool. One time the wife of Gam-lak-yeltq was at a fish-house with her four children when some Tse-tsauts saw her. One of them, named Ar-zen-nah, shot her. The bullet hit the strap of her pack and passed through her body, killing her. The pack fell to the ground and the baby was on top of the pack. A daughter, Tgax-dok, picked up the baby and fled, and a son, Ghaw-ghewh, ran away carrying the other baby, Gam-damas. (This Ghaw-ghewh was the grandfather of Mr. Peter Williams, Chief Gu-guł-gow.) As he ran, Ghaw-ghewh tripped and the baby fell from his back. He jumped up and kept going, leaving the baby there, and coming to the river he jumped in and floated down-stream. The Tse-tsauts found the baby and took it. They took the girl Tgax-dok captive and made her carry the baby. Meanwhile Ghaw-ghewh got out of the river and went to a place called Gwanksem-men-takqu, meaning "spring below a hill." Here he found a man cooling himself off at the spring; it was Ha-dak-gam-year ("ugly walker"), the man who had previously been hit on the chin by a bullet. The girl carrying the baby was very slow and it hindered the travelling speed of the Tse-tsauts. They made a rope of roots and hung the baby by the neck on a tree, where it was found later; then the girl travelled faster. This girl married into the Tse-tsaut people and had many children, who remember that they still belong to Kitwancool.

## PART TWO

Territories

of the

Kitwancool

## Territories of the Wolf Clan

Recorded October 13th, 1958, immediately after
the histories of the Wolf Clan totem-poles.

**The clan of the Wolves** owns 6 miles south of Kitwancool
along the road (to the 9-mile post from Kitwanga), the mountain named Wins-gad-du-masqu south-west of the village,
and all the lands, lakes, and mountains to the boundary-line
formed by Ks-gin-daa-hin Creek, which is west of the village.

On the east side of the Kitwancool Valley the territory of
the Wolves begins 6 miles south of the village, includes the
mountain Gwen-ga-nik (meaning "the sap of a tree," and so
named because it is shaped like the implement used to gather sap), and extends along the mountain approximately in a
north-south line to the 53-mile post on the north.

The Cranberry River north-west of the village is the boundary-line between the Wolf clan and the Frog clan. The Wolf
territory belongs to Chief Wee-kha and Chief Gwass-łam.

## 2

## Kitwancool Territories in General

(Immediately after the above in the manuscript is the
following statement of the total territory of the tribe.)

---

**There is a piece of territory** that starts at Mile 53 and goes on
beyond the Nass River, following the mountain ranges. It includes all tributaries flowing easterly into the Nass River and
west of Kinskuch River and north-westerly to Meziadin Lake,
thence northerly to the headwaters of the Cottonwood River
(Surveyor's Creek) near Bowser Lake, thence easterly beyond
the Nass to the top of the mountain range, thence southerly to a point 40 miles north of Kispiox on the Kispiox River
(the mountain which is the boundary is called Lip-ha-hut-quk),
thence southerly to the headwaters of Douglas Creek at the
mountain called Gwen-ga-nik, and thence westerly to the point
of commencement.

These boundary-lines take in all the trapping and hunting
territory of the Kitwancool people. The united power and title
of all this land belongs to the people of Kitwancool.

## 3

## Territories of Mah-ley Group
## of the Wolf Clan

(References to territories are made in the "History
of the Lands Belonging to Chief Neas-ła-ga-naws.")

---

## 4

## Territories of the Frog Clan

(References to territories are made in the
"History of the Totem-pole Ha-ne-lał-gag.")

## PART THREE

Laws and Customs

of the

kitwancool

# Laws Concerning Territories

---

**These are the laws** of the lands and hunting-grounds of the people of Kitwancool. The lands that belong to each clan hold the power for them. Another clan going on to these lands without permission would only make trouble. If a person of another clan was found on these lands without permission, his or her life would be taken.

Other people may be allowed to hunt there with the chief's permission if they go in company with the clan owning the hunting-ground. Anyone who marries into the clan may hunt there, with the chief's permission. If a woman marries out of her village she can go and hunt with her husband, but if she has children, they belong to Kitwancool, even if born and living somewhere else.

The chief gives the power over his hunting-grounds to his nephews, and they are free to use them. They have been given the power to rule these hunting-grounds belonging to their clan.

One of the strictest laws is that no hunting-ground can ever be cut in half and given to anyone. No one is allowed to make any such hunting-ground smaller or larger, even if they own or have power over it. This also applies to all fishing-grounds and all natural resources in and under the ground. This law is so severe and powerful that no one from another clan or without clan rights can come to hunt, fish, mine, cut timber, or do any other thing on these lands without the consent of the head chief and his council.

These laws go back thousands of years and have been handed down from one generation to another, and they must be held and protected at all costs by the people owning these lands. These laws are the constitutional laws, going back many thousands of years and are in full force today and forever.

**PRESIDENT**

In later years the title of president was bestowed on the man who was given the power to protect these laws. The first president under these laws was Chief Beeyosqu (Christian name Mr. Albert Douse), who died more than forty-five years ago. After that Mr. Albert Williams (Ne-yas-yal-lart), the father of Mr. Peter Williams, was the second president of Kitwancool. The third president is Mr. Peter Williams (Chief Gu-gut-gow). He was given the power and the right to protect these laws.

The village chiefs have put on him the power to see that all these laws are carried out. Any government laws sent out to Kitwancool will have to be examined by Mr. Peter Williams prior to their being presented by him to the village in the presence of the chiefs of the village. If anyone comes from another village to discuss this land law, Mr. Peter Williams would have to examine it before it would be allowed to be discussed.

These laws cover the natural resources and the erection of dams for water power and the taking of any minerals or oil out of the ground, or in any way interfering with the naturalness of the country. In any such case, anyone wishing to do this even by the consent of any government body must arrange a meeting with the president of this village, Mr. Peter Williams.

On the 14th day of October, 1938, all the chiefs and all the young men held a meeting in Kitwancool. They created a pact or law of agreement among the chiefs of the village, and this then formed a union between the Frog and Wolf clans. In other words, these clans united as one, and under this agreement they swear to protect all the lands and natural resources belonging to the people of Kitwancool. This agreement still holds good and will remain in effect until it is changed again (if ever it is changed) by another meeting of the chiefs and the villagers.

## 2

## Chieftainship, Rank, and Power

**One man is the head** of the Wolf clan of the village, the wise man Gwass-łam. Wee-kha is the second man at the head of the clan. These two men come out of the house of Gwass-łam.

The second house of power is Fred Good's house, Mah-ley. In case of trouble, war or famine, they send Mah-ley to the house of the two wise men to find out what is to be done, as they know how to handle it.

The chiefs are very particular about who wears their crests, ceremonial clothes, and masks, and each clan takes care of its own. If a clan made use of another's clothes, masks, and such things, it would always bring trouble.

When a clan raises a totem-pole and puts their rightful crests on the pole, it means a great deal to them, as every pole has a hunting-ground. They are very particular: a Wolf cannot hunt or trap on a Frog's grounds nor can a Frog go on a Wolf's grounds. To help put on this feast, the nephews go out to the territory and hunt. A chief who has many nephews and nieces is lucky. The rest of the clan also help. When the chief is going to his hunting-ground, he invites all his household to go with him, and also all the other households of the Wolf clan. They hunt only on the hunting-ground of their crest, until they have enough for the feast. The head of each household is the head hunter over that house.

When the chief of a clan dies, he is laid out awaiting burial. All his clan are there, as well as invited guests. They have a feast, called a feast to choose a new chief. They pick a young man whose life is clean and honest, a good provider, a man who is wise. This is done in the presence of the gathering at the big feast. All the chiefs agree that he is the right man to choose as a reigning chief. He takes the place and receives the name of the dead chief.

### SEATING

The chiefs are seated according to their rank. If it is a meeting of a single clan, such as the Wolves, the head chief always sits in the middle, with the second chief on his right, the third on his left, fourth on his right again, and so on for as many Wolf chiefs as there may be in the village. These men that sit on each side of the chief are his councilmen. Guests of high rank must sit where the chief tells them.

At some meetings or feasts the Frogs may be seated on one side and the Wolves on the other.

The seat in the middle of the back of the house, where the head chief sits, has the highest rank and power. The next highest chiefs sit on each side of him, according to the rank and power they hold, right around the sides to the door. The seats get lower in rank as you come from the chief's around to the door.

## SPEAKER

The chief never stands up, but has a man who stands up and speaks for him. He is also a chief, as a chief never asks a man of lower class than himself to speak for him. The first speaker of this house (the leading Frog house) is Chief We-dak-hai-yatzqu ("big copper") (a chief always owns a copper shield with his crest carved on it, and the bigger the chief, the bigger the copper). The second speaker is Chief Goa-gash ("one who speaks first").

The chief himself never talks. He just looks at his speaker, who knows what to say, having been given his instructions before the meeting. If there is serious trouble in the village and the speakers have failed to bring peace, then the chief is asked to speak and settle the matter.

# 3

## Chief's Costume

(*See* Plate 7.)

---

**This is very important.** Whenever there is trouble, the chief puts on his head-dress called am-a-lite. It has a carved wooden crest on the front, it is trimmed with ermine-skins, and its crown is filled with eagle-down (mek-gaik). He bows his head over the people so that the eagle-down falls on them, and this means friendship and peace. Whenever mek-gaik falls on you, you must be a peaceful person. When people of another village are invited to attend a feast, the chief dons his head-dress filled with eagle-down and dances a dance of welcome, spreading it over his visitors.

In the picture, such a head-dress is seen on Chief Wee-lezqu (right). His name means "big blue grouse" (the bird that is heard drumming on hollow logs and calling its girlfriend, omh-omh-omh). He carries his ceremonial-dance rattle in his right hand. On the fringe around the bottom of his dance apron can be seen the hoofs of unborn caribou. His blanket is a button blanket trimmed with ermine skins. The neck-piece he wears is made of woven cedar-bark and is called a lou-ith. It is trimmed with abalone-shells (bla-aa).

The head-dress on Chief Gwass-łam (left) is made of twist-
ed cedar-bark rope called gax-do-m-luk. Around his neck is a
lou-ith, and over his shoulders is a black-bear skin. His "rattle
apron" is trimmed with unborn-caribou hoofs and carries great
healing power.

PLATE 7. KITWANCOOL CHIEFS IN COSTUME, 1910.
LEFT: CHIEF GWASS-ŁAM. RIGHT: CHIEF WEE-LEZQU.
G.T. EMMONS PHOTOGRAPH. RBCM PN03928.

## Marriage

**A chief's daughter** must always marry a chief, because when she has children she takes the name and power of that chief. This same law exists in all the world among the whites of royal blood. The children of noble birth then become chiefs when the time comes. Indian girls are not allowed to marry until they are 18 years old, as before that they do not know enough to be married.

It is a very strict law that a chief is not allowed to marry a common woman. She must be a chief's daughter. If he were to marry a common woman, his children could never become chiefs.

If a man has picked out a girl be would like to marry, his family choose two or more women in good standing in their society and they take presents to the relatives of the girl. This is called mass-aws, meaning "decorations," and among the gifts are some decorations. They wait a few days, and if the presents are not returned, they know the man has been accepted. After a few more days they give presents to all the girl's relatives. (The first time, only the father, mother, and aunts of the girl received presents.)

The man's relatives then approach those of the girl with more presents, and following that a marriage feast is held, with all the big chiefs in attendance. The couple sit prominently at the back of the house. One by one the chiefs rise and give the newly married couple their advice as to how to carry on all through their lives, explaining to the woman that she must leave all her old boyfriends, and to the boy that he must never look at another girl. They tell them never to commit adultery, explaining that to look into another man's (or woman's) eyes could mean death.

5

## Naming of Children

**First ceremony:** For the naming of children there is a meeting to which all the villagers are invited as witnesses. Then Frog or Wolf chiefs call out the name of the child and the father presents gifts to all those who called out the name.

Second ceremony: A boy has a hole pierced in each ear by his aunt; a girl has a hole put through the lower part of her lip. Before this ceremony a boy has a child name or na-muk. After it he is called shak-gwee-qus. A little girl has a pet name called ark-gahs; after the hole is made in her lip she gets another name, na-argh. This is done only to chiefs' children, never to those of lower rank. These children who have the marks put on them will become chiefs later on in life.

Third ceremony: Now they will teach these children the songs and dances. The dance is called su-ha-lide. The chiefs file in and sit in their places of honour. Rattles are handed to them. The children are seated nearby. The chiefs stand, and with motions of their arms throw their power into the children. Each chief shakes his rattle and dances. Then they put the ceremonial head-dress on the child's head, with eagle-down in it. Another high chief, who must be a relation of the child, places a little eagle-down on each of the chiefs. The name of the performance is Su-ha-lide.

Fourth ceremony: When a boy has reached the age of maturity, they again call the chiefs together to a feast, at which presents are given around. The chiefs then confer a higher title on this shak-gwee-qus (child). Thus having gone through all the ceremonies, he is now a chief. He has the right to enter the feast-house and can receive gifts. On the death of one of his uncles he is now qualified to take his place, provided he is found worthy and has the consent of the council of the chiefs. Many people are never made chiefs and can never enter a feast-house when feasts are given. There are only so many chiefs allowed in a clan. On the death of a chief a shak-gwee-qus may be called in to make up the required number of chiefs.

When a feast is given in a village and a shak-gwee-qus is called in, he puts up all his wealth and divides it among all the chiefs of the village. This entitles him to go to other feasts. Before he can go to feasts in another village, however, he must give presents to all the chiefs of that village. After that he can attend all feasts. He does not have to give again, but if he wants to step up until he reaches the top, he gives things as presents to all the chiefs at every feast he attends. This makes him a great chief, if he is capable enough to be the successor of the head chief.

## Girls' Maturity, Boys' Maturity

**It is a law** that when girls reach the age of maturity (about 13 years old), they are put in little brush houses, where they must stay for ten days. These are a long distance from the fishing-grounds. The girls must not look on the fish or it would bring misfortune to the village. They have three cedar-bark ropes running to the fish-house. One they pull when they want water, one when they want firewood, and the third when they want food. They are never given fresh salmon to eat, only last year's cured salmon. They are not allowed to cross water, as it would offend the fish. When they drink water, it is always through a tube.

Men are not allowed to look at or pass near the huts, which are called welb-eryep, meaning "house of dirt" because it is dug into a hillside and has dirt on its roof. A grandmother always lives with the girls. If they have to go outside, they wear a large hood so that they cannot see the mountains. It would stop the fish if the mountains were angry. If they have to go in a canoe, their mouths are filled with stones to keep them from talking or laughing, else the spirits would fly away with them. Their condition makes them unclean; when they sleep they are not allowed to lie down, but must sleep sitting up. Other members of the household might have to lie there, and the unclean spot would not be good for them.

That starts their womanhood. After one season or year of that they become women. Girls who followed these rules lived a long time, much longer than those who did not. They were always strong and healthy. They also had good luck, and were always looked upon as women of good morals, good character, honour, and pride.

A boy cannot eat the muscle or the shoulder bones of any animal, or else his arrows will fail to kill whatever he shoots at, and he will get leg cramps while chasing game. He eats only from the neck and rib sections of an animal.

## Divorce, Widowhood

**Whenever a husband or wife** becomes unfaithful, going out with someone of the opposite sex, it is no longer considered fitting for them to live together. They separate at once, but neither is free to marry again until he or she fulfils another law called betqu, which means the same as divorce.

They must call the chiefs to assemble, as they did when they got married. The woman who is asking for the divorce (if it was the woman who called the chiefs together) stands at the back of the house in front of the chiefs. Sometimes she brings two or more relatives to stand on each side of her. She sings what is called betqu, a divorce song, and dances. Then she gives presents, as much as she can afford, to all the chiefs who attended, and to all her attendants.

While the woman is still dancing, the man who desires her burns something of great value to himself, as an indication that he is the man who wants her after she is free.

After this ceremony she is free to marry again. A man asking for a divorce must go through the same ceremony.

Widows and widowers blacken their faces, leaving a narrow strip of skin under the eyes to give the appearance of much weeping. Strangers then know they are widowed. If they are very sorry, they may keep the black paint on four years. Then they put up a feast to wash their faces, washing away their sorrows. They are then free to marry again. Some marry after one year, but if they marry in less than a year, bad luck always comes to them.

# 8

## Cooking

---

**Cooking was done** in a square box which had one seam in it, put together with wooden pegs. The fish or meat was put in it with water and cooked by dropping in red-hot stones. It was a slow method of cooking but it was used for many generations.

They also had roasting-sticks (an-yow). A salmon was roasted by sticking the sticks through it and into the ground and turning it once in a while before the fire. Meat was also done in the same manner. Up on the mountain when they kill a goat, they make a trench, line it with stones, cover this with leaves, and light a fire on the top. In about two hours the meat is cooked.

A fishing-pole is called maa-oo and looks like [three-pronged leister].

# / APPENDIX /

## 1. List of Names in the House of Chief Neas-ła-ga-naws

### CHIEFS

| | |
|---|---|
| Mah-ley | Like crazy man. |
| Neas-ła-ga-naws. | |
| Ak-gwen-dasqu | No one allowed to touch him. |
| Gal-lay | Outside noise. |
| Ge-de-gelxqu | Rope dragging and always catching on something. |
| As-de-wal | Accidentally. |
| Ks-sem-we-zean | Rat maiden. |
| Ha-youly | Fishing man. |
| Me-key-laa | Making lots of noise. |
| Ksem-we-len-get | Wealthy maiden. |
| Gek-zem-goal | Giant magic. |
| Giat-dem-get-wank | Whistling man. |
| Laa-gae | Bad talker. |

## ADULT WOMEN

| | |
|---|---|
| Ks-sem-hyda (Mary Good) | Haida woman. |
| Ks-sem-gaigh | Another Gets-skan woman. |
| Ks-sem-get-wass | Raining maiden. |
| Giss-will-japqu | Making herself different. |
| Git-wal-kem-ha | Strong wind. |
| Guk-dam-muk (Maggie) | Science woman. |
| Gwen-zaił. | |
| Nee-zeah-hal-mha | Grandmother. |

## BOYS

| | |
|---|---|
| Ak-de-an-muk-de | Messenger who tells nothing (trusted). |
| Kha-dep-belk | Flat part on head of frog. |
| Gam-dam-mast | Hugging but not kissing. |
| Gaw-gwah. | |
| Noo-you. | |
| Zam-moał. | In a fish trap. |
| Oaks-la | Swimming away from the shore. |
| Zex-al-al-ga-k | A bluffer. |
| Ak-de-ha-nu-omt-maxt | Something you throw in the water that doesn't die. |
| Ak-will-ga-gess-kqu | Never stops talking or making music. |
| Ks-sa-weal | To squeeze out. |
| Ks-sa-gomel | Turning your eyes only, to look. |
| Dec-am-omakqu | If you do not like them, do them no harm. |
| Gee-goah | Until tomorrow. |
| Ha-dak-gams-ga-lał | Badly spread out. |

## GIRLS

| | |
|---|---|
| Lu-tgal-daw (Rena Good) | Frozen on the ice. |
| Tgax-doak | Lying on the ground. |
| Ha-gwel-ga-gait | Plain or clean skins. |
| Ne-ks-clos-kug | Sunning itself on something. |
| Na-hud | Afraid in woods and runs into open place. |
| | |
| Da-gum-gaik | Twisting out of things. |
| Ak-goad | Never take him. |
| Sa-gap-goss | Jumping on trail in front of the house. |
| | |
| Lu-de-yansqu (Molly) | Mixing up wood with leaves. |
| At-tyem-mel (At-te-mel) | Not allowed to follow my example. |
| Nee-loak | On river rocks. |
| Gas-de-moatq (Easter) | Just recovered. |
| Le-guel | Eyebrows. |
| Ks-sim-mas-wazak | White otter maiden. |
| Ged-a-will-zapqu | Improves herself. |

## LAMENTATION, OR LEM-MIK-OIE

O-yea-ha-hay
Yo-oo-oo
Ah-ho-he-yo-loo
Oo-lo-he-yo-ha
You-gam-star-on-the-giat
He-yoa-lo-he-yo-loo
Oo-he-hay.

## 2. List of Names in the House
## of Chief Gwen-nue

### MEN

| | |
|---|---|
| Gwen-nue | Begging. |
| Az-jex | Proudly. |
| Go-gag | Little Raven. |
| Gogash | Firstly. |
| Ga-wa-garney | War, peace maker. |
| Gam-ktea | Bloody and frozen. |
| Geo-lu-ha-nag | Only women. |
| Gal-le-gwin-year | Travels upward. |
| He-win | Like a seagull. |
| Gaa-kl | Rat. |
| Giad-dim-speid-gan | Man of the woods. |
| Legi-gwan-dimks | Likely cut off. |
| Hud-dim-kqu | Bluffing, threatening. |
| Wit-tak-giat | Giant man. |
| Lig-gi-waik | Step heavily, sinking in snow. |
| Wee-an-ga-zen. | |
| Niss-san-hakst | Bunch of forces together. |
| Gam-sis-sag-gatq | Slowly crept. |

### BOYS

| | |
|---|---|
| Leg-ge-yim | Just smell. |
| Gis-goutqu | Landing-places. |
| Gal-luzh | Somewhere, shedding hair. |

| | |
|---|---|
| Ks-dam-gam-gaik | Sound of birds' wings. |
| Gwin-nak-nitqu | One who tells you where he is when you cannot see him. |
| We-łi-yie-ai | Looks like a spring salmon. |
| Gamk-dinah | Barking downwards. |
| Ya-ga-wok | Sleeps downhill. |
| Tka-muks | All ears. |
| Lu-laa-lak | All ripe fruit. |
| Twen-dik-lel-pt. | |
| Giss-yoks | Moving about and busy all the time. |
| Tka-na-kł | Bigger blackfish. |
| Kse-lok | Little mound on sea or river (humps of land the size of man's head). |
| Daakh | Excavated house. |
| Gwal-did-thou | Water freezing to paddle or poles. |
| Sta-bha | Man's or woman's thigh. |
| Gwis-nea-kł | Blanket or blackfish. |

## ADULT WOMEN

| | |
|---|---|
| Ak-goadim-gwel-lenget | Foolish slave or servant. |
| Gwas-gail-ł | Borrowing dishes, etc. all the time. |
| Mak-la-leaks | Barefoot traveller. |
| Nna-gan | When I hit you with a stick. |
| Gam-yagak-ous | Walking from a high place to eat dogs in a low place. |
| Ksem-mak-magie | Rainbow maid or woman (a dance goes with the name). |

Ks-sim-ha-gwel-zozs          Woman of a kindly bird.
Gan-gein-nems-giatqu         Like a man's track.

## GIRLS

Ghak-la-quq                  Tail dragging.
Ne-gam-mks                   Sun shining on.
Tga-hast                     Flat fireweeds.
Dak-oagk                     Heaving a rope or line on a copper.
Alu-nee-yatht                Kill each other openly.
Galey-ks-oat-qu              Silent dip of the paddle.
Oaks-hud                     Fleeing away from the shore.
Lu-his-yale                  Misleading, or taking the
                             wrong route.
Sik-gukt                     Trying to shoot a target.
Sag-ga-gaiks                 Making wings for themselves.
La-le-gen-isqu               Lowly grizzly bear.
Ya-ga-daah                   As you travel downward then
                             sit down.
Yas-daa                      Person who dies then comes back
                             to tell her heavenly story.
We-dak-ga-nak                Large black fin of the blackfish.
Zok-gam-ne-dah               Girl who was sitting on a log and
                             being pulled toward the shore.